Coping with
Crying
and Colic

an easy-to-follow guide

Siobhan Mulholland

Vermilion

Contents

Introduction

Crying is part of your newborn baby's language – it's his way of communicating. When your baby cries he is telling you how he feels and what he needs at that moment in time – if he's hungry, tired, or frightened. Your baby cries to let you know what's going on in his tiny little world and without this interaction you would find it much harder to look after him and to form a bond with him.

The good news is that as your baby gets older he will cry less and less because he will find other ways to communicate, and by the time he is a year old he may even be able to say the odd word. Every baby is different – some shed a lot of tears, others relatively few, but as any mother who has had more than one child will tell you, this is often more down to the baby than any radical difference in parenting technique! As a parent, you will soon learn what your baby's cries mean and how to soothe him, and this book has been written to help you do just that. Please note that to avoid confusion the baby has always been referred to as 'he' but this could just as easily have been 'she'.

Chapter 1

CRYING What you need to know

All babies cry – there would be something wrong with them if they didn't. How much they cry differs widely, but the average for a newborn is two hours each day – which includes the amount of time they spend fussing, sniffling, grizzling or crying inconsolably.

During the first hour after birth your baby may appear very alert. This will be short-lived as babies usually have a period of 24 hours or so, very soon after their birth, when they become intensely sleepy and not very interested in feeding. It is thought that this drowsiness is brought on by the physical effort of being born.

Crying phases

In his first few hours and days after the birth, your baby may be fairly quiet. He might sleep a lot of the time, just waking every few hours expecting to be fed. By the end of the first week, he will probably find his voice and start to cry more and more. During his first month the amount he cries will gradually increase, reaching a 'developmental crying peak' at six weeks. At this age your baby will probably cry for an average of 2–4 hours a day, much of it happening at the end of each day and in the evenings. By 10 weeks the worst is usually over; your baby should be more settled and learning other ways to communicate with you. By four or five months, your baby's crying and fussing will have stabilised to an average of around an hour a day; as he gets older, he will continue to cry less and less. By the time he is a year old he will have found lots of other ways to get your attention! However, do remember that all babies are different, and that this is only a guideline, so don't worry if your baby cries more or less. If you are particularly concerned, always seek advice from your health visitor.

Your relationship with your baby will also change during his first year – you will get to know him better and feel more able to predict what will make him cry and what will make him smile.

Communication

Although it will be at least a year before your baby says his first word, he can actually communicate very well from day one. He can communicate with you, your partner and definitely with any stranger who dares to pick him up.

Your baby will communicate in many different ways. When he is pleased to see you or excited he will jig about, moving his arms and legs frantically, as if performing some sort of dance. When he is fascinated by a beam of light playing on the side of his pram, or a mobile dangling over his cot, he will open

his eyes very wide and stare. And when he wants something: food, warmth, or a cuddle, he will cry in such an effective way that someone will usually be at his side within minutes.

Crying is the main form of communication for infants. In babies it is a reflex action in the same way as rooting for the breast and sucking. If your baby needs or wants something, he will cry: he will inhale air into his lungs sharply and then breathe out through his vocal cords making the sound of a cry.

Your baby's cry is the perfect 'signal' – it lets you know when help or assistance is needed. He is incapable of taking care of himself, so he has to get someone else to do things for him, and he communicates this by crying. When your baby cries he will be seeking a certain response, eliciting help from those around him to take care of him and very effectively ensuring his basic needs are met. In many ways your baby's survival depends on his ability to cry.

Ways of crying

Every baby is born with a distinctive voice, which you and others close to him will quickly come to recognise. In a room full of babies, you will be able to tell if it's your baby that is crying. You will also be able to tell by the pitch, constancy and duration of the cry how upset your baby is – whether he's crying because of something very urgent or just letting you know that he's there.

You will come to understand the difference between a low-level grizzle and a fabulous full-throttle bellow – and quickly be able to determine whether your baby is a bit tired and needs a nap, or is furiously hungry. Your baby will send out 'graded signals' through his crying – letting you know

TOP TIP
Remember, crying – especially in the first six months of his life – gives little indication of your baby's real temperament. Infant tears are not a reliable way of predicting future personality.

how he is feeling. You will not know the precise cause of his distress based purely on the sound of his crying – for instance there's no specific cry for hunger or for comfort – but you can get an indication of how bad things are, and by a process of elimination try to work out what might help. There may be patterns to your baby's crying that will help you – for example, if he's upset at certain times of the day more than others, if he screams before or after a feed, or if there is some particular activity like having a bath that provokes a furious response. Of course some of the time there may well be nothing 'wrong', he may still cry even if he is well fed, changed, rested and close to you. You will also come to recognise these periods of crying too.

CAN YOU SPOIL A BABY?

Your baby is bombarded by so much as he adapts to his new world and his needs, especially at the start, are great. He is very vulnerable and relies on you to be there all the time. By responding to this you are not spoiling him.

It is important to respond when your baby cries; a newborn should never be left to cry for longer than five minutes. Studies show that comforting young babies promptly, whenever they cry, may actually help to lessen their fussing and crying as they get older. After six months, some sleep-training methods do rely on a baby being left to cry for short periods.

Perhaps the best advice is to do what comes instinctively. If your instinct is to pick your baby up and comfort him whenever he cries, especially during his first few weeks, then do this. Remember, every baby is different; some will need more comforting, holding and nursing than others. Some babies – no matter what you do – will have periods of crying when they just can't be soothed. So try not to compare your baby with other newborns. You will come to know your baby better than anyone else and understand his temperament and his needs. If you find your baby's crying is in any way worrying, don't hesitate to seek advice from your health visitor or doctor.

Responding to crying

The constant cry of an infant is designed to be disturbing – nature has made it that way. It's a very difficult sound to ignore: strangers passing in the street will turn their heads, children will stop playing and look, grandmothers will start clucking, and if you are the mother of said baby you will find it very hard indeed to do nothing about it. In fact, a baby's cry can have such an effect on his mother that it can stimulate the 'let down' reflex if she is breastfeeding, causing her to leak milk from her breasts. Studies show that people find a baby's cry more distracting than something as irritating as 'low-level machine noise'. That's because we are hard-wired to respond. The sound of a baby crying evokes a biological response in us: it raises our blood pressure, increases our heart rate, changes the amount of blood flow to our skin and causes us to tense our muscles – in short it produces all the classic symptoms of anxiety and stress. We run to soothe a baby because in many ways it reduces our stress level as well as theirs!

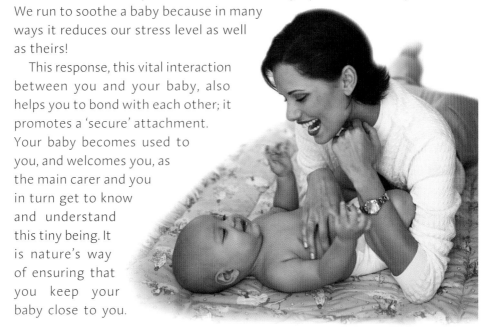

This response, this vital interaction between you and your baby, also helps you to bond with each other; it promotes a 'secure' attachment. Your baby becomes used to you, and welcomes you, as the main carer and you in turn get to know and understand this tiny being. It is nature's way of ensuring that you keep your baby close to you.

Chapter 2

WHY YOUR YOUNG BABY CRIES
Getting to know him

The reason why your baby cries will sometimes be obvious and sometimes will only be discovered by trial and error; there will also be times when you just won't know why he is crying. It will take time to work out what causes your baby to cry, so do be patient – you both have a lot to learn!

Your baby will cry more during his first three months than at any other time in his life, but at around 3–4 months you may find your baby needs significantly less soothing. The reasons why your baby cries will not have changed that much, but he will be less troubled by them. During his first six months you will find your baby gradually becomes more robust, more at ease with the world around him, and more easily assured that you are always close at hand.

He is hungry

One of the most common reasons why babies cry is hunger. Like all of us they do not like to go too long without food, but unlike older children and adults 'too long' is actually no time at all for young babies. Your newborn's stomach is very small, approximately the size of his fist, so his tiny tummy will need feeding little and often. In the first couple of weeks, your baby may only manage 2–3 hours between feeds and will let you know in no uncertain terms when it is time. Most babies cry much more before a feed than after it – so check if your baby is hungry before you do anything else. As well as crying, your baby may 'root' for milk – this reflex action happens if something touches his cheek, causing him to turn his head as if searching for a nipple. However, if your baby has just been fed and then starts crying, the cause is unlikely to be hunger.

He needs a nappy change

A wet or soiled nappy may make your baby cry, although you shouldn't rely on this as a sign that it needs changing as modern disposables can be particularly effective and your baby is unlikely to know he is wet. If you have just fed your baby, check his nappy next. If you leave a baby too long in a wet or dirty nappy, it may cause nappy rash. Symptoms vary from mild red spots to sore broken skin to, in extreme cases, blisters. The rash is a reaction to the ammonia found in urine; if your baby's delicate skin is exposed too long to ammonia it causes irritation. Nappy rash will cause your baby to cry so change his nappy frequently and as he gets older let him kick about for a short time every day without a nappy on.

He is too hot or too cold

Young babies have difficulty regulating their body temperature, during the day and at night. It will be some time before your newborn baby's internal thermostat can react to temperature change in the way yours can. If he's not dressed appropriately, and he's in a cold environment, he will struggle to keep warm; but if he is wearing too many clothes or has too much bedding on he will quickly feel hot and bothered. In both instances, he's likely to become fretful and cry. You can test your baby's temperature by feeling the back of his neck. There are also ways to stop him getting too hot or cold:

TOP TIP
Don't rush too much and get anxious when dressing and undressing your newborn as this might distress him further. Take your time and be reassured that you'll soon become so efficient, he won't have time to cry.

- When you are undressing your baby or giving him a bath, try and make sure you do so in the warmest room in the house and away from any cold draughts. When babies are undressed, they lose a lot of body heat quickly.

- In the first couple of months, dress your baby in a vest under his sleepsuit. If it's cold, put a cardigan on him as well. By the time he is two months old, your baby will not need to wear any more clothes when he's indoors than you do.

- The ideal temperature of the room your baby sleeps in should be 18°C (64°F). Never let him sleep with a hot-water bottle or electric blanket, or next to a radiator, heater or fire. Keep a thermometer in his room to help monitor the temperature.

- It's best to use lightweight sheets and blankets as bedding for your baby's cot or Moses basket as babies have a tendency to overheat. When their babies are around four months old some parents prefer to use a baby sleeping bag. These sleeveless bags can be zipped up to the neck providing a practical alternative to sheets and blankets which can be kicked off during the night.

- Do not use duvets, quilts, pillows, cot bumpers or anything 'frilly or fancy'. These are all thought to increase the risk of cot death, as young babies are unable to lift their heads and could suffocate if in contact with these sorts of bedding. They are also prone to overheat if sleeping under a duvet.

- Always keep an eye on the temperature of your baby – reduce the number of sheets and blankets if he gets too hot. On hot summer nights he may not need any covers at all.

- Put a hat on your baby if you are going outside in cold weather.

- If you put extra clothes on your baby for outdoors, always take them off again when you come back inside.

He is overtired
Young babies really can't cope with too much stimulation. It takes very little to overstimulate them: being kept awake too long, being handled by too many different people, or experiencing too many different, sudden noises, lights or voices. That's why Christmas day is always a bit of a challenge for the very young! An overtired baby needs to sleep and he should have no problem letting you know this – he will be irritable, fretful and fussy, and he may rub his eyes and cry. He may refuse to settle at first and find it difficult to sleep. If your baby is distressed by too much activity, take him to a quiet, dark room and gently soothe him in a calm environment.

TOP TIP
Learn how to soothe yourself. When your baby cries put on some calming music which you enjoy, make sure you eat healthy meals, phone another parent going through the same and 'share' the moment, do some deep breathing and relaxation exercises. And when your baby finally sleeps, make sure you do as well.

He needs to be held tight
Your baby has been in the very secure environment of your womb for several months and then suddenly, often within hours, he finds himself in a very different place. A place he can move about in, where there is a lot more noise, many strange vibrations and much more light. Exposure to the outside world can, at first, be very frightening and

daunting. This is why your baby, especially when he is newborn, needs a lot of intense, close physical contact. He needs to feel secure and warm. Sometimes this state of being can only be achieved in your arms. For some babies, a Moses basket or cot, however lovingly prepared, is just not the same. This is why your newborn may cry as soon as you put him down, yet stop crying as soon as you pick him up again. Many babies, especially in their first few days and weeks, feel happiest when they are physically close to someone.

He hates being undressed

It will take your baby a while to get used to being undressed. In the early weeks, for example, you might find it very awkward trying to get his tiny arms and legs in and out of a sleepsuit. However gently you go about it, the whole exercise will feel very alien to him. Babies much prefer to keep their clothes on – they like the feel of the material against their skin. So don't be surprised if your baby is able to predict when he is about to be undressed and promptly starts crying. Try covering him with a warm towel when you undress him, as he will find this comforting and enjoy the sensation of having something warm next to his skin.

He has had a fright

When a baby is frightened by something, if a noise or an unexpected movement or action suddenly startles him, he will react with jerky movements. He may fling his arms sideways with his fingers outstretched; he will then bring them back in slowly, clenching his fists. He will look very

> **FUSSY BABIES**
>
> Some babies need more hands-on care than others – they need more reassurance, more physical contact, more carrying and more rocking. If they don't get what they want, they cry until they are picked up and cuddled. You might find the only way to keep your baby happy is to keep him close and carry him around all the time, in a sling *(see page 28)*, a papoose or in your arms. This is not the type of baby you can put down for long, or who finds self-soothing *(see page 33)* easy.
>
> If you have a sensitive baby, remember that crying is a very natural part of being a baby and as long as he is healthy, feeding well, gaining weight and getting adequate sleep, you don't need to worry. Life usually gets a lot easier for sensitive babies as they get older – they do become more independent and robust.

surprised and start to cry. This is your baby displaying the Moro reflex – an involuntary action babies are born with which disappears as they mature. It's a reflex action that will happen while your baby is sleeping as well; he may twitch and jerk, often quite dramatically, causing him to wake up and cry. If this happens, pick him up and cuddle him, holding him close. Try swaddling him *(see pages 31–32)* before you put him back down to sleep as this may stop him waking himself again.

He has colic

The main symptom of colic *(see pages 35–41)* is crying on and off for several hours, or over one long stretch. These bouts of crying usually start in the late afternoon or early evening after a feed, and can go on until eleven or twelve at night when your baby (and you)

> **TOP TIP**
>
> Studies show that how 'good' a parent you are has little affect on stopping babies under the age of 3 months from crying for prolonged periods. So if you've tried everything to try and comfort your baby, then don't beat yourself up about it – these bouts of unexplained crying are not a reflection of your parenting skills.

fall into an exhausted sleep. A baby with colic is often very difficult to soothe. You can walk around with him, rock him gently, let him suck for comfort, try to feed him, but at times he will be inconsolable. There are no proven cures for colic but it does pass – by four months the majority of babies seem to recover and only in very few cases where there are sometimes other complications is it considered serious. Be reassured that if your baby has colic he will still thrive, but if you are in any way concerned do seek advice from your health visitor or GP.

He is in pain or is ill

When your baby is ill – when he has a cold, the flu or a tummy bug – you will know about it during the day and you will know about it during the night. Your baby will seek your reassurance regularly and need to be comforted. He will need much more love and attention than usual as he snuffles and coughs his way through his first bugs.

Your baby's symptoms may be loss of appetite, a runny or blocked nose, a cough, slight feverishness, sickness or diarrhoea – all of which will make him fret, grizzle and cry.

Young babies can become quite distressed when they have a cold and blocked nose, as they have yet to learn how to breathe comfortably through their mouths. If your baby has a blocked nose it might cause him to wake often during the night in a distressed state. He may also find it hard to feed, as sucking on a breast or bottle will be difficult for him if he is unable to breathe easily through his nose. It's therefore best to anticipate that, during the few days your baby has a cold, he will be very unsettled.

However, these types of minor illnesses usually last just 2–3 days. If you are at all worried about these symptoms – or if they persist – then you should call a doctor immediately.

He has reflux

This condition is linked to the immaturity of a baby's digestive system. It is effectively 'heartburn' and the pain from it will make a baby cry, especially after a feed. Reflux is caused when a baby regurgitates his feed repeatedly. If you

WHEN TO CONTACT YOUR DOCTOR

You know your baby better than anyone so always trust your instincts if you think your baby is ill. If his crying sounds in any way unusual and goes on for a long time then you are right to be concerned. If your baby is whimpering or screaming and you have checked everything – that he's not hungry, or too hot or too cold, etc. – and he can't be comforted or settled to sleep then talk to your pharmacist, GP or health visitor. Symptoms can progress very quickly with young babies so it's important to get them checked fast.

However, it's also important to remember that babies who are very ill often do not cry at all. For instance, if they have a fever they will probably sleep more than cry. A fever in a child occurs when his temperature is 38°C (100.4°F) or above. If your baby is under three months old and has a fever, you should contact your doctor immediately.

With older babies you should contact your doctor if the fever lasts for more than a day, or if you are at all worried about your baby's condition. Often a fever is accompanied by other symptoms such as vomiting, diarrhoea or a skin rash which are usually signs of an infection.

think your baby is suffering from reflux, consult your doctor. As with colic *(see page 18)*, the majority of babies outgrow reflux, and as long as a baby is putting on weight and otherwise healthy, it is not considered a serious problem.

TOP TIP

Many babies cry a little when they go to sleep, or when they wake up during the night. As your baby gets older try waiting a minute or two to see which way his crying goes. Often babies fuss and grizzle as they settle themselves to sleep – this is normal. So don't rush in immediately to comfort him, see if he can sort things out for himself. If he can't, he should have little problem letting you know!

He is growing and changing

There will be times when there is no obvious reason why your baby is crying – he's been fed, he's slept well, he's had a mellow, calm morning and yet he's started to become fractious and tearful. When this happens, you just have to accept that this is sometimes what young babies do. Research suggests that unexplained crying is linked to a stage of development that very young babies go through and it does not mean there is anything specifically 'wrong'.

Chapter 3

HOW TO COMFORT YOUR YOUNG BABY Practical techniques

Trying to find what will soothe your baby is a bit like working out how to bake the perfect cake. To start with you have to experiment a bit with all the ingredients, trying a bit of that with a bit of this, until you get the right mix. And so it is with babies. The best approach is to combine different techniques to discover which ones your baby finds most soothing. But do remember this is an ongoing exercise. As your baby develops and matures, so will his likes and dislikes, so, frustratingly for you, what worked one week may not do so a couple of months down the line.

Feed him

There is nothing as comforting to a young baby as a full stomach, so it's best to eliminate this option before anything else.

It isn't advisable to attempt a rigid feeding routine with a newborn baby – if you do, you are guaranteed a few tears! It is important that your newborn regains his birth weight fast, so feed him whenever he seems interested. Sometimes you can pre-empt the tears by looking for other clues that he is hungry, such as him rooting for a nipple or teat to suck on. When and how much your baby feeds will be fairly erratic – he may cry just an hour, or even half an hour, after a feed and then surprise you by feeding again. The way to avoid cries of hunger is to feed your young baby little and often. Start off by feeding him at least every 2– 3 hours, gradually extending the time between feeds as he gets older.

Cuddle and comfort him

All babies like to be held and cuddled by the people they know best. They enjoy the warmth from your body, they are reassured by the sound of your heartbeat and they feel secure being held tight in your arms. This is why a lot of babies do not like it when you put them down. They will demand, in no uncertain terms, to be picked up again and comforted in your arms.

For most parents it is totally instinctive to scoop their babies up in a warm embrace. It quickly becomes apparent that holding a baby close soothes the tears and that cuddling calms agitation. Research shows that you will benefit from this contact, too. The light touch and gentle pressure that comes with hugging your baby causes the release of oxytocin, sometimes called the 'cuddle hormone', which induces anti-stress effects such as lowering blood pressure, reducing anxiety and pain, and making you feel calm and relaxed. It makes everybody feel good – not just the person getting the hug, but the one giving it as well.

Babies need physical contact, which is why they seek it often by crying out for it. You will soon learn what your baby likes – and you may be surprised by how definite and particular he can be from very early on. Certain 'holding' positions quickly become favourites:

- Hold your baby upright, against your chest, so that he can look over your shoulder. He will like being held close to you and, once he can support his head, he will have an interesting view over your shoulder. It is also a good position for 'winding' your baby after a feed.

KANGAROO CARE

Very close contact is often used for premature babies in what is called 'kangaroo care'. Mothers, and increasingly fathers, are encouraged to spend several hours a day holding their premature babies skin-to-skin against their chest. This, amongst other things, helps maintain the baby's body temperature when he is not in the incubator.

- Hold your baby so that he is facing the same way as you. He will be upright with his back against your stomach and chest. Use both of your arms to support your young baby – one around his waist and one supporting him between the legs. But again, once your baby can support his head you can just keep one arm around his waist.

- Drape him over your arm. Hold him between his legs with his tummy resting along your arm and his head, face down, at your elbow. His arms and legs will naturally hang down. Many babies find this a very soothing position – they appear to enjoy the light pressure on the stomach. This is sometimes an effective technique for soothing colic (*see page 39*).

- Lay your baby across your lap, face down, and rub his back gently. He'll love this position and, again, it can sometimes be an effective way to soothe colic.

- Sit your baby up on your lap and support his neck and head with one hand, put your other hand on his back and gently rock him back and forth. Babies find rocking motions very calming and you'll soon find yourself getting into a natural rhythm.

Let him suck for comfort

Sometimes your baby will suck on your breast or a bottle for comfort rather than nourishment. He will stop crying as soon as he is offered a nipple or teat, latch on, but not actually feed. You could try giving your baby a dummy or encourage him to find his thumb, although there are some disadvantages to both.

PROS AND CONS OF DUMMIES AND THUMB SUCKING

DUMMIES

Pros
- Babies find sucking very comforting, so give your baby a dummy to suck on as this may help soothe him.
- Dummies are very safe, as it is impossible for a baby to choke on or swallow one. The teat of the dummy is made of silicone, rubber or latex and is attached to a plastic mouth shield.
- Dummies are easy to keep clean and can be sterilised in the same way as the teat of a bottle.
- Some parents find dummies effective in soothing the bouts of inconsolable crying associated with colic *(see page 36)*.
- There is some evidence that the use of a dummy may help protect against cot death – the reason why has yet to be fully established.

Cons
- Encouraging your baby to use a dummy may affect your chances of breastfeeding successfully, especially if your baby starts using a dummy during his first six weeks. When your baby sucks, he stimulates your breasts to produce milk. If you give him a dummy to suck on instead of your breast this may reduce your milk supply, which can then cause feeding problems.
- Some experts believe using a dummy can cause 'nipple confusion' – that is, your young baby may find it difficult to change between your nipple and the teat of a dummy.
- Studies show that babies who use dummies regularly are more likely to be weaned earlier, as they are breastfed for less time compared to babies who use dummies infrequently or not at all.
- Once your baby gets the hang of his dummy, it may be very difficult to get him to give up the habit.
- Although a dummy may help your baby soothe himself to sleep, if he loses it in his cot at night it will unsettle him. He may wake

up and cry, and he may not stop crying until you retrieve it for him.

● Frequent use of a dummy has been linked to an increased chance of ear and stomach infections in young babies.

● It's thought that dummy use may affect speech development. The ability to 'babble' is an important part of learning to talk, but if a baby regularly has a dummy in his mouth he may not be able to do this as often as babies who do not use dummies.

● Long-term use of a dummy may cause dental problems. Continuous sucking over a number of years may distort your child's 'bite'. This happens when the upper and lower teeth do not meet properly. Some experts believe that this is only a problem at 5–7 years of age – when a child's second or 'adult' teeth begin to appear.

THUMB SUCKING

Pros

● It's difficult to lose this comforter in the middle of the night or in a shopping centre!

● Some babies need little in the way of introduction to their thumb.

Cons

● Your baby is more likely to suffer problems with teeth alignment as a result of thumbsucking than if he uses a dummy.

● It can be more difficult to stop a child sucking his thumb than sucking a dummy. You can take your baby's dummy away but there's not much you can do to hide his thumb.

Rock him

Babies love the sensation of rhythmic movement, of being in constant motion. It is what they are used to as they've just spent months being swayed gently in the womb. Parents seem to instinctively know that this movement will soothe their baby. That's why you often see mothers with their young babies in their arms while swaying their hips, gently rocking back and forth, walking up and down and gently jiggling about. It's as if they are taking part in some deeply intuitive mother-and-baby dance routine.

This explains why rocking chairs and cribs have always been so popular, why pushing a baby in a pram is known to often bring an end to crying and why many parents swear that the only thing that will stop their baby's tears is to drive them around in a car.

TOP TIP

If you sense your baby wants to be close to you most of the time, then you could try carrying him around in a sling or a shawl. Not only will your baby be soothed by being close to you but you will also have your hands free. Parents of 'fussy' babies (see page 18) say this is a particularly effective way of calming them.

Pat and stroke him

Gently patting or stroking your baby on his back or bottom can be done while standing up with your baby against your chest or when you put your baby face down across your knee. Babies do seem to be reassured by what are often no more than light rhythmic taps and strokes. Some people claim it reminds babies of the sound and feeling of their mother's heartbeat while in the womb.

Massage him

Evidence shows that in healthy full-term babies massage can help to reduce crying levels. The good news is that you don't have to learn complicated techniques. In fact, you probably already massage your baby every day without realising it; for example, when you run your finger up and down his cheek or arm a few times you are actually massaging him.

If your baby does not respond positively to being massaged, simply try again another time, perhaps when he is calmer. Massaging tends to work better between feeds, rather than immediately before or after one.

TOP TIP
If your baby becomes distressed when he is naked, simply massage him through his vest or sleepsuit instead.

How to massage your baby:

- Make sure everything is warm: the room, your hands, and the baby oil if you choose to use it. Remember babies feel the cold very easily *(see page 14– 15)* and they don't like it.

- Lay your baby down on a towel in front of you, or on your lap.

- Keep eye contact with him throughout and talk or coo away in a gentle, quiet voice.

- Start by lightly stroking your baby's hands and fingers and then move onto his feet and toes.

- Next stroke his arms and legs – moving your fingers up and down a few times with a little more pressure than previously.

- Stroke your baby's torso either by moving your fingers up and down or in smooth circular movements.

- Very gently stroke his neck and forehead.

- If your baby looks like he's losing interest or if, having soothed his crying, he starts to fret again, then stop the massage.

Sing to him

Contrary to what your grandmother might have told you, babies actually like noise. Not the sudden, startling type like a car horn or an alarm going off, but the everyday hustle and bustle sounds that go on in every household. They find low-level background noise soothing – especially 'white noise' like the sound of a vacuum cleaner, or a radio blaring away, or a tumble drier whirring in the background. Babies, in particular newborns, are not used to silence – the womb is not a very quiet place!

This is why babies also love to be sung to, and why the lullaby, to be sung in a low, soft voice, was invented. It is perhaps the oldest trick in the book to settle a baby by singing to him while rocking him to sleep. But if crooning isn't your thing, put on a calming tape or CD to fill in the unfamiliar silence. Even the sound of your voice gently talking away will be a comfort to your baby.

> **TOP TIP**
> You will no doubt be given a lot of advice by well-meaning friends and relatives – but remember all babies are different and just because one mother swears by singing all the verses of 'Hush Little Baby' every night, it might not necessarily work for your baby.

Play with him

As your baby gets older, he will stay awake longer and need more stimulation. Sometimes he may grizzle for no other reason than he's a bit bored and needs some entertainment. If you think this is what may be wrong with him, then provide a few distractions:

- Attach a mobile to your baby's cot. Your baby can hear from birth and will be intrigued by noise, so the tunes that mobiles play will captivate him. If the mobile is a moving one, it will also attract your baby's attention.

- Try putting your baby under a baby gym. Babies quickly learn that if they 'act', certain toys will 'react', that the mirrors, soft toys and rattles hanging down from the arches of the gym do different things. They will try to bat things with their arms and kick with their legs.

At around three months, attach a rattle to your baby's wrist. He will be fascinated by his ability to make a sound when he moves At four months, your baby will be able to grasp and shake a rattle.

Your baby can see colour from birth, but can't distinguish between shades, such as red and orange. Until he's around two months old, he will respond better to contrasting shades, such as black and white. After this time, bright colours will appeal to him – so make sure he's surrounded by lots of colourful toys and books.

Place your baby on his tummy and surround him with colourful toys. Start by putting the toys within reach so he can practise grasping. Then put them out of reach so he will attempt to move to get to them. Make sure he doesn't get too frustrated, though.

A newborn will only need a few minutes of stimulation at a time, but a six-month-old can keep going for half an hour.

Swaddle him

'Swaddling' your baby means wrapping him up tightly in a shawl or cellular blanket in such a way that his arms are kept firmly by his sides, with only his head uncovered. Newborns have a very strong Moro reflex *(see pages 17–18)* that causes them to twitch and jerk. These sudden movements often startle infants, causing them to wake up from their sleep and cry. By swaddling a baby you are lessening the effect of these involuntary actions and some experts believe that by copying the restrictive conditions in the womb you are helping your baby feel more secure.

How to swaddle your baby

● To reduce the risk of cot death it is recommended that you only use thin materials for swaddling. Make a triangle shape out of a shawl or large cellular blanket and put it down on a flat surface like a bed.

● While your baby is still awake lay him on the blanket. Make sure his neck is level with the longest edge of your triangle and that his head is the only part of his body not resting on the blanket.

● Next, take hold of the right-hand corner of the blanket. Bring it across your baby's body, tucking it tightly under his right arm.

● Take the left corner, fold it across your baby making sure his left arm is wrapped up in the blanket, and then tuck it underneath him. Never cover your baby's head.

● Tuck the end of the blanket firmly under your baby's feet.

Leaving your baby to settle himself

Sometimes nothing you do will soothe your baby. You can put on an all-singing and all-dancing performance in soothing techniques and it won't make a jot of difference. There are times when your baby may start crying for no apparent reason and continue to cry. He may well be inconsolable for up to two hours – either crying continuously or on and off at random.

You know your baby, so trust your instinct. If nothing seems to be working, try tucking him up safely in his cot and leaving him on his own for a few minutes to see if he can sort it out for himself. Remember when this sort of

SEEKING HELP

If you feel your baby's crying is getting too much for you then you must take a break, either by leaving him on his own for a few minutes or getting another responsible adult to help out. Call someone – a friend, your partner or a neighbour, and see if they can help. Talk to your GP, health visitor, or Cry-sis – a self-help group for carers *(see page 6T)*. Never injure or shake your baby.

'unexplained' crying happens you are not the cause of it and often not the remedy either. It has nothing to do with your ability as a parent and your baby is not doing it to manipulate you.

Common concerns

Am I harming my baby if I leave him to cry sometimes?

The experts are divided on this subject. Some believe that with older babies – those over the age of six months – leaving them to cry for certain periods of time is absolutely fine as long as all their needs have been met. Others disagree, believing it can potentially harm babies in the long term.

What they do all agree on, however, is that a newborn baby should never be left to cry for more than a few minutes and this should only be the case if he is well fed, with a clean nappy on, in a safe place that is not too hot or cold, and if he is near to you. Babies this age need a lot of tender loving care, they need to know that you are there and they need to feel physically close to you at all times. However, when you've tried every other means of consoling your baby, tucking an overtired infant up safely in his cot or Moses basket, to see if he's better left alone for just a few minutes, may be a good move.

Why does my baby cry so much during and after feeds, he sometimes even appears to be screaming?

Your baby may have 'reflux'. This is very common in babies under one year old and occurs when their stomach content (food and stomach acid) flows back up into the oesophagus. This causes a burning sensation – similar to heartburn in adults – and often much discomfort, hence your baby might appear to be 'screaming' after feeds. You may notice other reflux symptoms such as vomiting or posseting, repeated hiccups, coughing, refusing to feed or only feeding for short bursts, and disturbed sleep.

In the majority of babies this is not serious and gets better by itself. As babies mature, the junction between their stomach and oesophagus gets stronger making reflux less likely to occur. Many parents report a marked improvement at around seven months when their babies are able to sit upright and eat solids.

In the meantime there are simple things you can do to alleviate some of the discomfort. Avoid overfeeding your baby by feeding him less but more often. Make these feeds as calm and quiet as possible. Try winding your baby and holding him upright after each feed for around 20 minutes. Never 'play' with your baby after feeding, as jiggling or bouncing him about may exacerbate his discomfort.

Chapter 4

What you can do

Colic is the name given to a collection of different symptoms that occur in very young babies at around the same age. It is not an illness, you can't 'catch' it, it lasts for no longer than approximately eight weeks, and it has no long-term effects. Colic occurs in infants with a normal weight gain, who appear healthy in every other way. If your baby has colic, it's very unlikely to be because of a medical reason; in fact some experts believe that if there is a medical cause to your baby's crying then he does not have colic.

What is colic?

Colic is often defined by the 'rule of three': a baby has colic if he fusses or cries for more than three hours a day, for more than three days a week, for more than three weeks. Give or take a few hours or weeks, millions of babies fit this diagnosis: they experience bouts of unexplained and inconsolable crying that start when they are 2–3 weeks old and last until they are around three months.

Colic is found in babies from all cultures around the world. The Chinese call it 'the hundred days crying'.

Signs and symptoms

The following signs are associated with colic:

● Bouts of inconsolable crying, irritability and fussing that often stop and start without warning and have no obvious cause. They can last for hours.

● The crying tends to happen in the late afternoon or evening and can last anything from 30 minutes to 4 hours, after which your baby (and probably you as well!) will fall asleep. In some rare cases crying can last all day.

● It usually starts in babies around three weeks old. They start crying and fussing for longer periods each day until they are six weeks old, when their crying peaks. After this the periods of crying gradually lessen. Colic usually disappears when a baby is 3–4 months old.

● Colic occurs in both breastfed and bottle-fed babies. It does not appear to run in families and is not affected by birth order – a first-born and third-born child have an equal chance of developing colic.

● It may seem as if your baby has a tummy ache, because while he is crying, he will draw his knees up over his stomach, maybe clench his fists, and sometimes arch his back and become agitated.

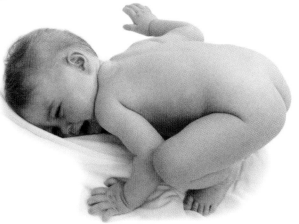

● Your baby will 'fuss' a lot: he may seek a nipple or teat only to reject it once he has it in his mouth; he may appear to want to be carried yet seem uncomfortable in every position you put him in; or it may look like he's very tired, but clearly sleep is the last thing he seems able to achieve.

> **TOP TIP**
> It helps to remember that colic only lasts for around two months and that it may actually be more upsetting for you than your baby.

● Colic appears to get better by itself – with no intervention from parents or the medical profession.

The causes

Over the decades a lot of different things have been blamed for causing colic: giving your baby too much or too little stimulation; tensions in the home; eating chocolate, onions or drinking tea when breastfeeding; not feeding your baby enough; feeding your baby too much; feeding your baby too fast or too slow; feeding your baby on demand; sticking to a schedule and feeding your baby every four hours; picking your baby up too much and spoiling him; or letting your baby cry on his own in his cot for too long. To say it's been a confusing debate for a lot of mothers is an understatement!

The one hypothesis that did stick for a while is that colic was brought on by digestive problems, by a baby's immature gastrointestinal system. Colic was thought to be caused by trapped wind in a baby's gut. And you can see why this might be if you look at one of the symptoms of colic: babies drawing up their knees as if they have an acute stomach ache.

> **TOP TIP**
> Remember, you are not alone. Join a mother and baby group or talk to other mothers of young babies, you will be surprised how many are going through the same thing.

The argument has now shifted again, this time away from the gut to the brain. Experts now believe – perhaps to the relief of millions of parents – that the type of prolonged inconsolable crying associated with colic is an entirely normal part of human development. That there is nothing 'wrong' with your baby when he is wailing like this and that he is not actually trying to let you know that there is. In fact all your baby may be doing is merely venting – crying for the sake of it and finding it difficult to stop crying once he's started. A six-week-old baby's nervous system still has a very long way to go before it manages to regulate much of his behaviour – your baby's crying is therefore a reflection of this immaturity and his temporary inability to stop crying.

> **TOP TIP**
> Try not to worry too much if your baby has colic. All medical evidence shows that although it may look as if a baby with colic is in great pain, he is not actually. His heart rate remains normal and his cortisol levels – a chemical in the blood that is used as an indicator of stress – are normal.

What you can do

There are no proven cures for colic. Some parents swear by traditional remedies such as gripe water, while others claim it makes no difference. Some breastfeeding mothers say a change in their diet helps, some say they see no improvement.

It may help to keep a 'colic diary', to note down the time each day when your baby's bouts of crying start and when they stop. It will help you prepare for that period of the day, to get all chores out of the way beforehand and maybe to ask if a relative or friend can come round to help. Also keep track of the different things you do to try to soothe your baby. This diary can also be a useful record if you need to talk to your health visitor or doctor. If something does appear to bring comfort to your baby, then repeat it every day.

Try holding your baby in different positions to see if this will ease his crying – for instance laying your baby across your knees face down and gently stroking his back, or laying him along your arm, on his tummy with his head at your elbow. It's thought the gentle pressure this exerts on a baby's stomach can be soothing.

Try rocking your baby, singing to him, patting, stroking or massaging him *(see pages 28–30)*. Try these techniques in isolation first and then in different combinations.

Try moving him to a calm environment: keep the lights low, play soothing music and do not have any visitors.

Apply gentle heat to your baby's tummy – for instance hold a covered hot-water bottle containing warm water against his stomach.

A change of scene can be as good as a rest; take your baby outside in his pram or in a sling *(see page 28)*. Both of you may find the outdoors distracting.

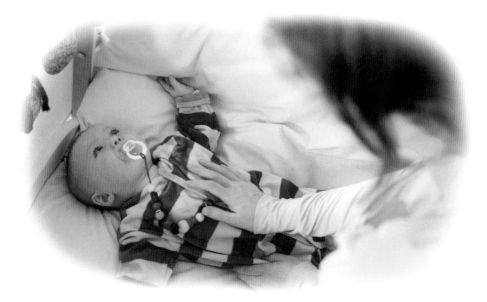

 If nothing else appears to be soothe your baby, then tuck him up safely in his cot or Moses basket and pat him gently on his stomach to see if he'll stop crying or go to sleep. If this does not help then leave the room and let him cry for a few minutes to see if he settles himself *(see page 33)*.

WHEN TO CALL THE DOCTOR

If you are worried about the sound, duration or frequency of your baby's crying, talk to your health visitor or GP. Show them your 'colic diary' *(see page 38)* as it will help them identify whether there is a cause for concern. Also note down times and duration of feeds if you are breastfeeding, or the amount he is taking if you are bottle-feeding, and your baby's bowel movements. It helps to have as much detail as possible.

If your baby is not putting on weight and if he is off his feeds, talk to your doctor or health visitor immediately.

If you find the crying too much and if you are feeling depressed, it is very important that you talk to your doctor or health visitor. They will have a lot of experience with babies with colic and the effect this can have on parents.

Common concerns

If I am stressed and tense will this make my baby's crying worse?

It might do. Some experts believe that babies can sense when their parents are tense and that this may, in turn, increase their distress. But it's a bit of a chicken and egg situation, as often a baby's crying – especially the inconsolable and unexplained variety – is the cause of a parent's stress.

If this is the case and you are finding your baby's crying very wearing and tiring (which many parents do), then see if someone else can help out. If you are finding it difficult to soothe your baby see if your partner, a relative, or a friend would be willing to take your baby for a while. Often, having a 'fresh' pair of arms for just half an hour helps enormously. This will give you time to have a nap or a bath or to get out of the house on your own, which should help you calm down.

If you are on your own then try taking your baby for a walk, either in his pram or in a sling. Often just getting outside helps, as it's a welcome distraction for both of you. If you can't face going outside then try tucking your crying baby up safely in his cot, turning all the lights off and leaving him there for a few minutes while you both have some 'time out' on your own *(see page 33)*.

And remember, as your baby gets older you will find that he cries less and less, so life for both of you will get a little easier.

Chapter 5

As your baby gets older, he will cry less and for fewer hours each day. He will become more interested in the outside world, more social and able to do so much more. But then you may find that your baby cries for different reasons. His rapid development will continue at the same ferocious pace, opening up different opportunities for tears. He will take to the floor and explore more, crawling, maybe even walking, and he'll definitely fall over sometimes.

He will become more of an individual, aware of what's going on around him, and at times be very frightened by it. If you were blessed with a peaceful baby who gurgled in the background for the first six months of his life, you might at this stage find that you are the proud parent of a baby with a truly boisterous bellow!

He is bored

At this age your baby will be spending longer periods awake. As a newborn he was awake for an average of 8 hours out of 24 hours, dispersed randomly throughout the day and night, and much of it spent feeding. By six months your baby may be awake for 10 out of 24 hours, mostly during the day and he will not need to feed so frequently. This means he has a lot more time so will need occupying for longer. At 6–7 months, your baby may be capable of sitting unsupported and his hand–eye coordination will be almost as good as yours. He is programmed to put all these newfound skills to good use and will be raring to go, so if he is not given the opportunity to do things you might find he cries out of sheer boredom. He might become particularly bored if he is:

- Left in his cot with nothing to do, with no toys and no mobile to look at.

- On a long car journey.

- Stuck in the same room for too long.

- On his own for a long time.

He is frustrated

With this quest for new experiences comes a lot of frustration. Your baby, sitting up unsupported, will start to reach out for things: toys, keys, the remote control, absolutely anything he can get his hands on and put in his mouth. In attempting to do this, he will undoubtedly have moments of real frustration. As he lunges forward from his sitting position in an attempt to pick things up he is likely to fall flat on his tummy a few times – each time with a loud cry. As he begins to yank himself up by gripping onto furniture or the side of his cot he may momentarily stand before tottering over with a magnificent scream. And as he starts crawling and staggering around your living room like an unguided missile he will start hearing the word 'no' a lot. Just you watch those howls of protest as you tell him what he can and cannot do!

He has hurt himself

It is inevitable that when your baby first starts moving around it will end in tears – usually his tears. Although it's very important to child-proof your home *(see page 56)*, you cannot possibly plan for every eventuality and part of any learning process is being allowed to make mistakes. So brace yourself for black eyes, bumps and bruises, and maybe even the odd split lip. When your baby first starts to hurt himself, he will probably scream very loudly – the volume of his cries will no doubt be out of all proportion to the scale of the injury. He will cry loudly not only because he has hurt himself, but also because he has had a bad fright. It is natural and healthy for him to protest like this. But if your baby knocks his head quite badly – for example, if he rolls off the bed onto a wooden floor, or falls backwards onto a coffee table while trying to stand – but doesn't cry, contact your doctor immediately.

TOP TIP
Some children learn caution fairly quickly, others seem to have to endure a fair few hard knocks before they get there. Remember it is all part of the process and that in order to learn how to walk your baby also has to learn how not to fall. He will get there in the end.

He is anxious and insecure

At around six months, your baby will start showing signs of 'separation anxiety'. He will begin to make it clear that he doesn't like it when you are not around. He will cry when you leave the room and seem more 'clingy' than usual; he will literally not want you out of his sight. And it's around this age that he will show that he really does not like strangers. He will cry if someone he doesn't know very well picks him up, or if he's left in a room with unfamiliar people.

Separation anxiety is a very normal part of your baby's development – it shows he is becoming more aware of who he is, and who you are,

and that there might just be a difference! But it also means it could become difficult to leave him with other people or to settle him in his cot to sleep. He may want you there by his side and become distressed if this does not happen, and fast. Any separation from you will cause your baby anxiety, whether it happens during the day or night. This anxiety may last for several months.

This is the time when a lot of things will start to frighten your baby, things that never appeared to bother him before. The sound of a vacuum cleaner – something he was once reassured by – may now startle him, a deep voice of someone at the door may make him scream, and seemingly benign activities, like having a jumper taken off, will bring on the tears.

He is over-tired

Don't let your baby get carried away with himself and his newfound skills. As your baby becomes older, more alert and more social, it's easy to forget that he can also be easily overstimulated by what goes on around him. Check your baby is getting the right amount of sleep for his age, especially the correct number of naps. Watch out for signs of tiredness: rubbing eyes, irritability, fussing and crying. And watch out for family occasions like birthdays and Christmas – they often end in tears.

He is teething

A few babies are born with teeth, but for most others their first ones start to appear between five and nine months (but if there is still no sign of a first tooth by the time your baby is a year old there is no need to worry). Teething affects babies differently. Some babies seem hardly bothered by it, whereas others find it hard going and can be irritable. Teething can cause increased dribbling, swollen gums, a desire to suck more than usual and occasionally a slightly raised temperature. This may well make your baby more grizzly and tearful than usual, but it will only be for a few days, not weeks. Talk to your pharmacist about this as there are many different types of teething rings and gels available which may help.

He is ill

With older babies you should contact your doctor if a fever lasts for more than a day, or if you are at all worried by your baby's condition. Often a fever is accompanied by other symptoms, such as vomiting, diarrhoea or a skin rash which are usually signs of an infection.

He is hungry

Your baby is older now, a lot bigger, doing more, and no doubt eating more. At six months babies are weaned onto solid food, and with good reason: they need the extra calories as they start to crawl and move about. Your baby's appetite will steadily increase over the next six months, and, as he has done since he was a newborn, he will let you know when he's hungry by crying. If you are not sure if his tears are caused by hunger, watch out for other signs as well:

- He puts his hands near his mouth, or he puts them in his mouth and starts sucking and chewing them.

- He starts sucking on his clothing or toys.

- He becomes fretful and grizzly before his next feed or meal.

- He starts crying for more milk after feeds or looks as if he wants to eat more after finishing his portion of solids.

- He starts waking up earlier in the mornings.

When your baby starts out on solid food, he may cry at mealtimes purely because he does not like the taste or texture of what he's being fed and he may miss his usual milk feed. This will pass.

He has lost his comforter

As babies get older they start adopting 'comforters' to help them get to sleep and make them feel secure. They may enjoy holding a favourite cuddly toy or a sad-looking piece of blanket. These 'transitional objects' are to be welcomed as they help babies soothe themselves. The only drawback is if they lose them, either in the middle of the night, or somewhere in the house or – perhaps the worst-case scenario – while they are out in their pram. The screams of outrage when this happens can be impressive, so be prepared for every eventuality – try to ensure you have a back-up one-eyed teddy.

Common concerns

My baby cries every time I leave him with the childminder. What can I do to make it less distressing?

This is a very normal reaction. Babies do not like strangers and do not like being left on their own with them. This is especially so after six months of age when your baby will start experiencing separation anxiety *(see pages 45-46)*. At around seven months you will notice that your baby does not like it when you leave him, even if it's just to go into the next room.

So the best approach with a childminder, or nanny, is to make them less of a stranger. Allow time for your baby to get to know this person. Try being in the same room or house as this new person and your baby, spending a couple of hours like this each day for several days. Gradually build up the period of time you leave your baby with this person.

Babies like routine, so form a predictable sequence of events for when you leave your baby with his childminder or nanny, in the same way you would at bedtime.

Always say goodbye and use the same phrases each time you do it – your baby will not understand the meaning of the words, but he'll come to understand the tone and sentiment of what you are saying. If your baby has a comfort toy, or blanket, have that at hand and make sure the way you depart each day is the same – be it by gradual withdrawal or a gentle, swift exist.

Your baby will soon come to understand that you do always return. And as he becomes more familiar with this new carer he will cry for less and less time after your departure.

NIGHT CRYING

It's always a bit of a shock to parents whose babies have been 'good' sleepers, to find that everything changes at around six months – their once perfect sleepers start crying during the night. There could be several reasons for this:

- Separation anxiety *(see pages 45-46)*. Your baby will wake up and want you by his side regardless of what time of the night or day it is. He may, for the first time, need you there to help him fall back to sleep again.

- It is around this time that your baby will first discover the ability to roll over. He will learn to move around his cot, maybe knocking into the sides, waking himself up and crying in the process.

- Your baby may also scream for your help to find a lost teddy or dummy in those oh-so-early hours of the morning.

- Your baby's increasing mobility may cause a few problems. For example, when he is supposed to be lying down peacefully in his cot, you might find your baby standing up and crying. At 8–10 months your baby might be able to pull himself up with the help of the bars at the side of his cot. Getting back down again is a different matter though, so he may need frequent middle-of-the-night assistance from you.

Chapter 6

HOW TO SOOTHE YOUR OLDER BABY Practical techniques

As your baby grows older you will find it much easier to interpret his crying because you know him better and you understand his temperament, and what upsets him and makes him smile. It will also be easier because your baby will be able to communicate his needs to you in many different ways: as well as crying, he will use facial expressions, gestures and body language. Also, the way your baby cries will have changed, it will be more intentional and specific – he will use it more to 'signal' his likes and dislikes. It will therefore be easier to work out how to stop him crying.

Give him toys

Babies are pre-programmed to learn to go on specific journeys of discovery using every sense in their body. Everything they come into contact with gets touched, felt, put in their mouth, sniffed, shaken about, pushed over, stared at, gawped at and listened to. It's how the very young take in information and attempt to understand the world, seizing every opportunity to do so. They will demand as many learning experiences as they can get and become easily bored *(see page 44)* and cry if they don't get the stimulation they need. This is why they love a good toy!

- Make sure the toys you choose for your baby are age-appropriate so that he benefits from them fully. Toys for older babies are designed to stimulate the senses that are key to this stage of development: sight, touch and smell.

- Surrounding your baby with lots of touchy-feely objects encourages reaching out and grasping – especially if such toys make noises easily. Bright colours will appeal and different textures will prolong interest.

- Put lots of blocks in front of your baby. From six months babies can pass bricks from one hand to the other, so large soft blocks can be used for building. Babies also enjoy squeezing and throwing them.

- Pots and pans, cardboard boxes, measuring cups – babies love them all. Often babies are more interested in the box and its wrapping than the gift that came in it.

- Soft balls are very good for helping your baby learn about cause and effect – if you touch the ball, it rolls. Put a brightly coloured ball just beyond your baby's reach to encourage him to reach out or creep forward on his tummy, or roll over and stretch.

Give him your attention

Your baby will get more stimulation from you than anyone or anything else. Your baby will learn more through interaction from you and other main carers than from books, television or being left on his own with toys. You can help him realise what a fascinating world there is out there, and that the more he engages in it, the less he will need to cry.

Your baby will be stimulated by just being around you, by watching what you do and where you go. A supermarket trip will be totally riveting, your friends will be fascinating and a trip to the park will be a real treat.

TOP TIP

Your baby will like nothing better than to watch the world go by. Sit him up safely, and supported, and let him look out of the window to see what's going on outside.

Reassure him

As your baby starts showing signs of separation anxiety *(see page 45–46)*, you need to be there to reassure him. This means a lot of comfort, hugs, cuddles and calm talking. Start saying phrases like 'I'll be back soon'. Your baby will not

FEEDING YOUR BABY

Starting on solids is a big step, but by six months most babies are usually more than ready for them. It is important to get the portions right, as your baby has a small stomach and, compared to you, can still only cope with being fed little and often. Watch very carefully how much you give your baby during his first few feeds – a teaspoon is a large quantity for him and although he may take the food easily, if he has too much too early he will fret and cry. So start off small and build up gradually. As your baby becomes used to eating solids, use any crying around mealtimes as a guide to how hungry he is and the portion size he can cope with. Bear in mind that he might sometimes cry because he doesn't like the taste or texture of the food, or isn't used to it. Don't force your baby to eat something he doesn't like, just try again another time – babies sometimes just take a while to get used to a new food.

understand the meaning of the words, but he will come to recognise your tone of voice and associate the words with reassurance of your return.

Try to be patient as he goes through this stage of anxiety. Never put him in the arms of someone he doesn't know, or leave him in a room with strangers. If he starts holding on to a favourite toy *(see page 48)*, then encourage it, as this is his comforter, his 'transitional object', which he knows is not going anywhere.

Distract him

Saying 'Oh, look!' is a great way of distracting a tearful baby and making him forget about being upset. You can point out a train passing, a plane in the sky, something on the television. If you appear interested in something, your baby will follow your lead. Grab something that makes an unusual noise that will stop him fretting. If you are out and about, grab a set of keys and shake them vigorously. Your baby's natural curiosity may get the better of him.

If you tell your baby he can't have or do something, he's likely to start crying. Pre-empt this by distracting him instead: for example, start playing a

 game that calls for a bit of interaction such as 'Peek-a-boo' or 'Pat-a-cake'. By playing the same game over and over again, your baby will learn to expect what's coming and enjoy it all the more. Or bellow out those classics like 'The wheels on the bus' or 'Round and round the garden'.

Cuddle him

Your baby will still need a lot of hugs and cuddles from you. As he explores and discovers more of the world around him, he will become more fearful. He needs your constant reassurance, physically as well as verbally, to let him know it's all okay. When he cries, he's probably looking for a cuddle to make him feel better. By giving your baby a lot of physical affection, you are creating a close bond with him and helping him feel confident and loved – this will help him to

be more independent and eventually realise that the world is not such a scary place after all.

How to protect your home and baby

One of the things you and your baby have in common is that you are both on a steep learning curve. For your baby it's all about bombarding every sense he has, while for you it's learning how to protect your baby from overload and injury. Until you see your baby crawling and staggering around your kitchen, you will not realise just how many accidents are waiting to happen.

Making your home a safer place is a must, not only because it will protect your baby but also because it will give you peace of mind to let him roam around.

- Put anything potentially hazardous out of your baby's reach: medicines, cleaning products, electrical appliances, etc.

- Install covers on your wall sockets and safety catches on your drawers and cupboards. You can buy plastic covers for the sharp edges of furniture, like the corners of your coffee table.

- Get down to ground level, look up and see what your baby can see. You will then get an insight into just how tempting his world is: knives hanging over the edge of work surfaces, kettle leads dangling and lots of small objects to be picked up and swallowed. This is an ongoing process, as your baby's skills and abilities develop fast – so what was safe one week may be easily in reach after a couple of months.

The most common accident for babies this age is tumbling over as they learn to stand or walk. As they fall down they are likely to hit things like a table, or get a bang on the head while crawling around the floor. Some accidents you just can't anticipate, so just make sure you are on hand to comfort and soothe.

TOP TIP
Remember, if you visit other people's houses they will not be child-proofed like yours, so do be extra vigilant.

NIGHT WAKING AND CRYING

If your baby associates falling asleep with you – if you cuddle him, rock him in your arms, lie down beside him or let him fall asleep while feeding – then he will expect exactly the same treatment every time he tries to fall asleep, which could be several times a night. Babies have short sleep cycles and they wake briefly as they move from one cycle to the next. So if during one of these awakenings something has changed since he first went to sleep, your baby will let you know – he will cry out for you.

Having the wrong sleep associations is the biggest cause of sleep problems for babies and young children. So now is the time to start changing these associations and attempting to 'shape' your baby's sleep patterns. When you have finished the bedtime routine and put your baby down in his cot to sleep, it's important that he's awake. That way he will learn to go to sleep by himself. He may not like this at first, and protest vigorously, but it will help him to eventually learn the right sleep associations.

Conclusion

There is no universal magic trick or special formula that will stop your baby crying but there are proven ways to help soothe babies. There have been remarkably few 'discoveries' about how to stop a baby crying – popular remedies such as calming a baby by rocking and patting him were invented a very long time ago. This may be because babies are meant to cry and we are not really meant to stop them, especially when they are very young. We can only comfort them and let them know they are not alone.

You are not alone either; millions of parents around the world have to cope each day with babies who cry for hours at a time. Remember, crying doesn't last, your baby will soon find other ways of interacting with the world around him. It might also be comforting to know that a baby's cry is never as bad as it sounds. Often babies are not in pain or suffering when they cry, although whether you could say the same for their parents is another matter!

USEFUL ORGANISATIONS

The Association for Post-Natal Illness
145 Dawes Road
Fulham
London SW6 7EB
Helpline: 020 7386 0868
Website: www.apni.org
Provides support to mothers suffering from post-natal illness and works towards increasing public awareness of the illness.

Cry-sis
BM Cry-sis
London WC1N 3XX
Helpline: 08451 228669
Website: www.cry-sis.org.uk
A charity providing self-help and support to families with excessively crying, sleepless and demanding babies.

Gingerbread
307 Borough High Street
London SE1 1JH
Helpline: 0800 018 5026
Website: www.gingerbread.org.uk
Provides support services and a self-help network to ensure lone-parent families do not have to face challenges alone.

Home-Start
2 Salisbury Road
Leicester
Leicestershire LE1 7QR
Phone: 0116 233 9955
Website: www.home-start.org.uk
An organisation that has a network of 15,000 trained parent volunteers who support parents struggling to cope. This can be for many different reasons: post-natal illness, disability, bereavement, the illness of a parent or child, or social isolation.

Meet-A-Mum Association (MAMA)
54 Lillington Road
Radstock
BA3 3NR
Helpline: 0845 120 3746
(7pm - 10pm, weekdays only)
Website: www.mama.co.uk
Provides friendship and support to all mothers and mothers-to-be, especially those feeling lonely or isolated after the birth of a baby or moving to a new area. By attending a local MAMA group, mums become part of a network of women wanting to make new friends and support each other through good times and bad.

The National Childbirth Trust
Alexandra House
Oldham Terrace
Acton
London W3 6NH
General enquiry line: 0870 770 3236
Breastfeeding line: 0870 444 8708
(9am to 6pm, seven days a week)
To talk to a qualified breastfeeding
counsellor about breastfeeding.
Website: www.nct.org.uk
Antenatal and postnatal classes
giving information and help to
mothers, including help with
breastfeeding.

Parentline Plus
520 Highgate Studios
53–79 Highgate Road
Kentish Town
London NW5 1TL
Phone: 0808 800 2222
Website: www.parentlineplus.org.uk
A national charity that works for,
and with, parents.

Tamba
2 The Willows
Gardner Road
Guildford GU1 4PG
Phone: 0870 770 3305
Website: www.tamba.org.uk
A nationwide UK charity providing
information and mutual support
networks for families of twins,
triplets and more.

INDEX

1 3 5 7 9 10 8 6 4 2

Published in 2008 by Vermilion, an imprint of Ebury Publishing

A Random House Group Company

The Random House Group Limited Reg. No. 954009

Addresses for companies within the Random House Group can be found at www.randomhouse.co.uk

A CIP catalogue record for this book is available from the British Library

The Random House Group Limited makes every effort to ensure that the papers used in our books are made from trees that have been legally sourced from well-managed and credibly certified forests. Our paper procurement policy can be found on www.rbooks.co.uk/environment

To buy books by your favourite authors and register for offers visit www.rbooks.co.uk

Printed and bound in Singapore by Tien Wah Press

ISBN 9780091923440

Please note that conversions to imperial weights and measures are suitable equivalents and not exact.

The information given in this book should not be treated as a substitute for qualified medical advice; always consult a medical practitioner. Neither the author nor the publisher can be held responsible for any loss or claim arising out of the use, or misuse, of the suggestions made or the failure to take medical advice.